waterways series

tunth-sk

releasing new voices, revealing new perspectives

tunth-sk

waterways
www.waterways-publishing.com
an imprint of flipped eye publishing

ISBN-13: 978-1-905233-31-1

Editorial work for this book was supported by the Arts Council of England.

The text is typeset in Palatino from Linotype GmbH.

LOTTERY FUNDED

for Flora and Tom, my Yes & Yes

tunth-sk

Emma Hammond
2011

tunth-sk

italics in the page list represent first lines

a constant flow of
traffic over and through
mine indent
what has been called

Personality today is
a slice of dreadfully tough
cough-gunk

in a soup of cuticles – it's
OK though you know
typical and as usual
another *ding dong day!*

sprite I rise then
see that which must be done
through wasps
put a few of them back in
the old barnet to begin
open my hand and find
a fruit
nestling and twirling in there

how
Poetic I thought
that I should have Produce there
and keep onwards stoic like
what is advised – keeping my
Paternally endorsed upper lip trundling
under a bit

I get in my plastic ball
and roll around for a while

these Pig-trough black cries squeeze out from them:

you must really try to stay linear dear
you're so
Privileged you see
and you've such nice hair...

Ѭ

A small tug on my forelock
at the sweetshop lady

a sheela na gig hands me the small change
and slips a chocolate orange in me

Stumbling out I reflect on the fact
that it's all rather painful really

and I go home to open myself outwards
to the computer

Later when I go for milk
the swallows make a pattern for me

a vast tapestry of flapping
like a bomb that casts birds on me

I watch them crashing down
and after a time it comes to me

nothing touches me right
nothing gets in my hair like a death doesn't

and this landscape
full of liars
has got nothing to do with me

i was never a girl guide and
brownies was
for losers –
i had my own club
it was the 'kiss my slug
none of you cunts can join' club
and only me and the omnipods
were allowed in

our cookery badge was mud in water patties
and fern lick bits of
dried clay
in a sauce of marshmallow charcoal spray
or crunchy darkling fresh shrimp brûlée
which we sold door-to-door in packets – tied
with gobstring & hedgehog spikes
NO ONE got away

i was in a league of my own with my
deadcow bones and granny's jewellery
hidden in the split-to-bits tree
drawing god as a fat man
telescope hard and probing –
i had him under control within the hour
there was no contest
a slug on each shoulder and he buckled
like a girl

skimming the frothy horse's sick
from the river with a spatula to take
to the air-raid shelter –
mixing it up with the vole skin silk
talking to each other in spastic voices
those were the days my friend no fret
or this silence crept up after sex
our
science badge
the little mice in traps wriggling
pin-eye done for
mauled by the teeth
and those larger ones for badgers
MOTHERFUCKERS that took your leg off

a vague notion then that my fat man
was a sweat-drop farmer in a lumberjack shirt
screaming red-faced and grunting
as the last drop was squeezed out
rosettes jostling in display for dressage
while a sad shotgun grease wife
up to the elbows in chickenspit giblets
packed the stuffing in

it was all so very cold
those whirlies flipping
on the just-ploughed field
coughing and that squeaking
in the air under their shells
lobster-loud in the pink tea-time sky –

there were tears and a whinny
someone shouting my friends
back into their boxes

there were worlds within the fire
my stragglywet hair in coils around
the goosebumps
a sense of horror and my sister hovered
in her brown uniform
a lightning bolt of yellow wrapped round her neck –
and silence such as you have never heard
as they untied the barbed wire from my thigh

you know when
something awful happens
they rip whole houses down
and the neighbours feel
better

there where it all happened

the chop chop of bodies
and leaking fat
onto the swirly rug
which had got to hurt

two and a half prostitutes
in the lift top fridge
and one more under the
floorboards

packed flat in bubble wrap
with perhaps only one half
of her breasts

and some frost where it
has entered

her poor unreliable door

i have this collar and up it
rises around my head like
a ruffle. i am a ruffle.
it is a fashion halo. i am fashion

ed. girlcore.
we pushes the dough into
a diva. washed-up i certainly am

not! i can hold my own
hem. up round my ears. there's
my frillies.

but don't shout about it.
sit with your skirt firm
over your knees. don't be *needy*,

learn about their passions. rage –

find out what makes them tick.
put on yr suspense belt.
keep it all tucked safe in yr
filofax.

be sistrly to yrself
and blood like cupcake mix
on your licky tissue
will follow.

you open your mouth into a yawp,
gaffer it up and hit yourself
with a tuning fork. grnnn

did your mother not?
you suckle on and tell us
the results. we are winning you say –
our team.

i turn sideways in the mirror to check
my belly. it's still there.
i think to myself *i am a landslide,*
bright as a butcher's window.

Trains would make him think of death
The empty people-less sort which flitted across
With Tiffany lamps and that blank white
Shriek as the brakes broke and they drew back

Of launching between the carriages like some dark
Springing monkey and on down to the track into
A handy bone-crush hold-all of blood
Let square as if in vacuum pack or a done-in car

Of witnesses then who shtick a grief-lite show
A thousand phone calls later (pleased and vital
But slightly inconvenienced by the bus)
Thrilled to see how kind this punctured Mr was

A glittering piece of real life folk
Who somehow in that place apart from day
Could still feel nothing and enough
To resist the force unravelling him

you keep coming back
in a different guise.
first you were blonde with
the curly wurlies,
but now you're dark with
bloody lips and
a geographic tongue.

next you're bound to be
shimmery, so far
a blood-fluke that ghosts
inside me and talks me up.
i will be beautiful
for 0.5 seconds
in a wrist-grip called wow.

we will drink spaghetti and cry.
i'll be crime scene tape
wrapped round your head –
your eyes will be eggs
smashed into girls
from car windows.

you can tell me your
ronald mcdonalds,
and i will slice you
with the letter knife.
one moment you will think
i am the one but the next
you will think i am not
the one.

i'm rotting in front of you
of course. you undo my
bra with one hand,
i think that's new.
if i close my eyes
i feel all the mouths
and punctures
that ever were –
my skin, dreadful with joy.

half a

your shock is a big dark dream –
words take you outward i have sin it.
sin it.

the position you occupy is one of
someplace.
you say poetry & i do.

where i am not
whittling you take the
pocket knife and pocket

it. deep in your warlock apron

twisting
on yr pitchfork.
i wouldn't put it

in the past you
held this walnut with
cc'd fingers

and cracked it 'til out came
fireworks
of tired trumpets.

we go upward on and in my
dreams you appear
entirely.

i hesitate to say that we
wouldn wouldn't would
i hesitate

too. say! we may be
two sides of the same
groin –

ze portcullis, la reine

Rob dropped me off in his big white car
my classical civilisation imminent
and underneath my big white shirt
his name in semi-permanent marker
adorned my stomach
a secret that the other girls screamed at
the smell of chum and more besides
white musk clinging at the edges
my pen racing through an essay
like a roman following his nose
as the crow flies

Well how was I to know about
the girl at the beach
a pint of water over my head
and him calling me stupid then?
his big dark empty house on a cul-de-sac
his mother a big white witch
writing his name on a rizla
legs like a greyhound and twice as fast
the hum from the refrigerator
and where he took me to
the bridge where that boy jumped
onto the into the not there

So there I was in the back garden
as brown as I could be and every hair
plucked cleverly
but you wouldn't come back until the funeral
4 years in the city and twice as proud
with me and my hair all inbetween
and mussed with clips and fluffed and sad
and my only shoes too high
and my only black dress far too short
for this whole thing and that
casket...
something stirred in there
imperceptible

That day and the next I sat on the station
in stark heat my bare feet
pounding
here where you dropped me off
remembering the way you smelt
of fish and chips a duckling
our
walk in the snow and me
taking a shit in the woods
as careful and precise as a surgeon
the way you sneered as you said
which one of the men at this table
have you not slept with?
and me
laughing at the insult like a child

꓅

i ran into an industrial estate and looked around,
the spikes got me.

i opened my eyes to the exchange rate –
it was no good.

i have drunk all the drinks
and told in bars of past dead singers and
cotton pickers' slave chests.

you have fallen off the world and gone,
in pictures you look vague.

but i've been stuck in worse elevators
with dry fishing dreams
of the great wide open –

and if i could take my spear and run it
into your body, i would.

Sleeveless Errand

my ma and pa did me well they
made me from twigs mud
splinters and stars but THEN
one day sent me away to buy some tartan paint
and that was that
i never saw them again

but it was their loss in the end
my mother had a black pudding for a nose
and by that time dad was not looking too well either
but it was all irrelevant to me
i was on my way to iceland in my
little blue boat
her virgin voyage from where i saw my
bloodied knickers float away

the nights got cold and the unicorn
was not so warm then
my sou'wester got thin as skin and wettened
by the spray
but in the days the rainbow fish jumped up
and settled on my tongue
'til land an isle of crust
came took me to my cave

that space of light
the flat pink flowers
strange to me as company
the sound of the ocean like
a green tongue trellised into me
and the roaring became me
as if it were of me

and i walked to the forest to make
shoes of the cones
a small man came out and handed
me carbon paper
i made rubbings of his hands and used
them as a map to get back
where a gull brought news that my parents
were done for

i milked the gull and he flew off
the milk in a pitcher under my bed
i was hiding it from the unicorn because i knew how he got
besides a lot of his fur had come off by then
and he was barely recognizable

丸

Outside at the cotton factory
spring is solid
and aeroplanes fly through it like fish

The canary islands are far away
a seizure written on them

I don't know my cousins
but I remember doing drugs in a car with Johnny
P

A stray tuft from the flight path
and the chainsaw says
That I'm alive and cold
but I have all my limbs at least

The tree I can see
I translate it for you –
it has a swagger I don't like

hex key: mascara wand

1

your hip is an iceberg
a face cut from golden mean
a + b is to a as a is to b
i smell you and you're
scotland

2

your fingers
drill dreams to me
as i fiddle with your laurels
your hex key
eyes my mascara wand
in confusion

3

soldiered to death
i put a flag in you
like a big strawberry
– you grasp my hand
and place it
inside myself
by your lack of absence

i have seen you open
here and there in rpm
silently gold in your smiling
and olden as raining

so gone to the shops
in my tweed sarcophagus
if there in the capsule
unclosing
you'd be
would i know you?

and are you over-priced
and over-ripe of dreaming?
is your face clean/
can i inspect yr legs/
are you suspicious of roads –
as endless?

an elk bright
pylon by the fire
straddling the scrapes and injuries
of a life designed for wondering –
your hand is the side of me
steeped in gristly

ghost-coloured flowers

and i am this to you:
hundreds and hundreds of cheering
a brand new
brown paper wrapped overlord
warm liquid agar

the smell of the railway
an underwater castle door
girl
sharpened knife

and more –
like a peculiar blue-eyed horizon

Induction Day

what a load of and
pointless slips out from my
brain
but never from my slipstream

silent struggles with the
projection until the purple arrows
spring outward –
almost into my food chain if you will

I have a chat in the break once
about carveries
and go back to my book

from their eyes I see
a little raisin lady
wearing her name on my chest

cleaving the words
hard into the wood
as a smith might

animals

when i go
underneath
i am a
spoke
like lightning into sky
i cuts it
open with a silver
aching

for i'm old
but some hills are
worse
and i'm vexed
in a mess of blood
and pulp
yet still

made clear by the
tiny crocuses and
sheaves
scattered upon my breast
like the refraction
of
light
on water

sudden and insistent
as a day –
you send me to the animals
with your kissing

One of many white ladies
I was a lily in the lake as
my skirts billowed outward
and I boarded the boat to
coast the shore to land.

There in the dark punishing spray,
I was bloated as a whale
with the light of Jesus Christ
illuminating me
(for which I praised The Lord
in this time of transgression that had befallen me).

The sound of the oar sweeping across water
like air rushing in and out of the chapel's pipe organ,
bringing me out of the sleepy eyed stupor I had found myself in
as we left my warded chamber.

My wet pantaloons clinging now to my poor bruised flesh
like ghostly hands reaching in to cover
my pale white skin,
like the night the men had come to me in the pantry
and daddy screaming from his sick bed
like no other noise I ever heard.

Filbert Crow Jones would take my sin and rinse the devil out,
his fine strong faith
would replace my stain
like the veil my mother had worn to the chapel
since our shame had spread around the ministry
like one of Golgotha Jack's ignitions –
his toothless cackle wild as
when the flames delivered the Wesleyan child
unto Our Lord that night in June.

And as we reached the landing
I could have sworn I saw an angel
risen up from behind the fishing boats,
his creek water eye
yellow crawling with the spawn
of a Mississippi catfish,
rolling round like a tumbling weed
and winking, winking, winking...

ㄍ

beyond the disc cast by a lamp
i'm tucked into shadow
neat as a bat
on a clean bed of green flat
felt

legs folded all
rain-grappling quiet –
a lighter left bright in a pool
outside

my feminine hygiene out of sight –
a leopard print dripping down the throw
and downstairs hardened
laughter like feet

the plastic sheet rustles

my position shown in sweat
is a body ringed right round

a, b, c, d, e, f, g, h, i love

i click-clacked down amhurst
tea-sure like alphabet st
was written by me

like wonderwoman i was
and every boy
wondered, wondered

why i smelt like
sex and who i was
sex in the sex with

well, i'll tell you for
free (i surely am)
and no mistake

i was in the sex with
this new shining black-
haired top we

shall refer to as 'magic'
hot and soft as
profiteroles

sparking through my days
like a crackle and
BANG

with the trickling red
fire and dark brown
kissings each

one round and smooth as
a mortar and then the
pestle what

kills me up
and opens me in bits
you bites my lips in

ouch and thanks
and cup me up and siphon it
won't you

come and have a go
if you think
you're

your love
like architecture has me
stuck sore-necked in awe –
love that is
so old somedays
it has almost died out;

like chivalry
was real as war was
or unreal sure,
a sentiment
better bladdered across
a field
(a proof that life
can end is all
they're looking for)
and there it is in death.

people have them up
like puppets saying
not done,
they shake the rattling
sleeves of dirt
and stir the crow
into a new black ceiling
of stars,
grief-struck for all they
never knew about
love

until now
when the now has gone,
and love belongs
to larger worlds of when

never touched upon,
and small and simple blessed
as a man.

tusks

cone-warm in my palm,
your eye fits snug and blinks
like sun through packed-in trees.

if i close it then i can walk your whole
(your woodland in my red boots
grows out my world).

your ivy finds my sockets
and lit-up glades of pink –
the tiny bones that make up feet.

my fingers reach to nest you.
tangled in ringless branches
your hair

is tusks

ᚥ

from a dark white sky
you fell into
my snowy body
like sun

at the window of my
ice hotel

the pools of your face.
i see them widening
like burst banks
of deep sky-brown.

i'm dreaming i like
the softnesses
of you,
your mouth hand-pink
in mine,

the stretches of fleece
that untundra me.
i tip

the stone cold nights
riverward to the fish
that sink to see me
shivering;

as opening elsewhere
like sunrise,

you bring out your flint
to unfurl me
in the blue orange flame
of your fire

Blue Chinese Trees

Keeping circle tight in the teashop
with the finger puppets in pockets and
sickle cell fudgy animal shapes
crackling in packets all sweet and smug
i'm
intimate with a scone
twiddling it like a dial on a safe round
my plate with the blue chinese trees

Old Betsy suspects I am skate-like
she keeps her eye on the pond and that
twitchy swan what got me breadless
its hard cuttlefish peck beak smiling
and big eye (a whales) the whites
of a washing line are flags which say
surrender, you know!

Well maybe I am not cut out for this kind
of cricket on the green and Constable bow wow –
what if I were a cut above a pirate like
a big raw cutlass-mouth of teeth
blackened by sea-spray and drinking my poor old Mum's
blood in a goblet or something?

Officer Daley past the window on a broom rings his bell now
Hello Betsy what's for afters today? he croons
Betsy swoons and stumbles like a racehorse landing badly
Well it's your favourite sir
I found the jewellery at the back of my box she adds
and squints at me all purple-veined and knobbly
all special and unconcerned I've only had one cream tea
my whole life this morning

And its drizzly but that's the England I know
that's the spirit blank as walks in woods on Sundays
the smell of uncles kissing you like dragons
and smokeless coal the first snowdrop that *chancer*
like a hard white hand clawing out from
the earth into a photograph
written onto the world by light

I've come past all this I'm washed up lost not
as bad as Betsy but headed that way even she can see it
she gives me another scone all kindly when happy talk
comes on the wireless
there's more than an ounce of twinkle
left in that one yet but I have to look away when I catch a
glimpse of her stocking top
of her on the officer saying *is it in yet sir?*

Instead I watch a train in the distance
puffing over the big green hill
full of men in bowler hats
coming back to the crossword
and Phileas dog
coming back toward slipper and pipe,
the flagstones cold as frozen
and a wife as warm as a body.

Photographing Snowflakes

for Wilson Bentley

I look down at my mittens
as you begin to photograph me.

You touch my face a little and move my cheek to the side,
red against white with the dog barking.

A compound microscope, you say,
and a tiny beam of light entering through the small aperture.

You sit me down on a stile and arrange my hair,
the heavy orange sun around you like a coat.

When a snowflake melts, the design is lost forever.

A lens dangles free in your cold white hand,
you rise it slow to your face.

You sigh, peering at me with your strange glass eye.

We had one storm last winter which brought me
perhaps the most interesting snow crystal I have ever seen:
a wonderful little splinter of ice, incredibly fragile,

and broken –

when I think of it, it makes me almost cry, even now.

Ж

wide as snow
and covered by explorers
we were lost in a 2-minute silent mouthful
of icy cold water

i dove down through the murkiness
and found the red wet lantern
dim-shining as a box of lamp-light
on the dusty floor of a barn

did my eskimo spells on you
while you tied me up with a carrick bend

said goodbye to birds and snipers
the green skinned snake
(lung-heavy with skimming stones, stars
the dark low moan of a tanker
and the rest of it)
and let the water out

later, your moccasined feet
left damp footprints in the hallway
and up the stairs

i didn't hear you come in but found a bit
of seaweed by the toaster
and a long burgundy scream in the fridge
which i threw out into the snow for the owls

꒙

your wonky eye
stops you
from seeing
my redness

i have a
flat hand
with crumbs on
for your peck peck peck

the gaps in you
keep me 7-and-a-half
with a mouth full of twigs

while in other news
your LOL and ROFL
bird my heart out of the ground

И

I am in the baby-grow
and you have on the lion mask.
My feet dangling out the ends
and two eyes in the gaps are marbles.
Your whiskers shiver at me,
there are holes in the Terry towelling.

You wear the cossack's hat
and I have the visor
casting a pink cheek over mine.
I watch you being round
and can't not watch you fiddling.

You check a country on the map
then put a finger in my mouth
to mark the location.
My hand underneath you
spills the beans,
I worship your cow-lick and lick it.

You are in the silver suit.
I think you are on the moon.
I pick up the scissors to trim you,
I call you frond.
I stick out my tongue
and catch your scrummy tears.

ᚼ

deep in the moss
you covered in dew –
this terrible crush
has claws and teeth
for snapping
the bracken
in two

your mouth:

a soft hole in the
tall grasses by the silo

your body:

a silver birch bark
timber dragon
i fly around on

金

golden in your skin
with lips just opening to the sea
you're a channel

and gone back
to the depths where all the
snapping fish say how do

your face
a world of lions
is secreted away
to where i wake myself in laughing

and i stop to not think of it –
your body
burnt onto mine
like a hole in my thinking

for the man of transparencies
that you may be
i think you could not be aware
of how barley in the wind
you have made me

see, you unwind my splicing
as you arc from the sea

and i am no longer in this poem
for you have killed me

丙

you are as white and rough
as a piece of toast

when i bite into you
there is a crunch
and i get jam on my cheek

modern dance

i looked down at my size 5s. i saw what he meant –
my feet were cold and dead like i was already on
the slab. my toenail had been ripped off and was painted
green. i once considered that kooky, but now i am dead and all
that has no discernible meaning anymore.

i thought i may get to this point hand-in-hand, and still think i
     might –
yet the piercing loud tunnel from earlier dreams
makes me lose out. those able-bodied kissings come and go,
but essentially i am all alone and dreadful.

later on i am probably asleep, bogged down in some thinkings.
i will be dreaming about my scar that runs from hip to hip.
my fingers will trace it like a blind man, confuse it for a straight
     mouth.
more than anything it is just another wall that puts its hand up at
those that try to scale it.

a head came out of it once and i felt it.
i walked my own footsteps in blood and the nurse came with a
     nappy
to clean it up. i lay in my own filth and watched
modern dance on a silent tv. a man lifted a woman as slight as air
and trapped her in a flickering basin.

you came and camped on my nightie and lit your gorgeous fire.
in this forest of trees i hear your voice in every clearing that our
     bodies made.
somewhere across the fields is a caravan brown as flasked tea,
where i put on my record with the singing birds and try to call you
     home.

Ж

it seems to have been years
i never wanted you
in skin
entirely made
from tired

a spark we have
like space
and your eyes
a tunnel to it

i found you in
blood
and saw more
in you than any

of the love
that never was

like a wing on a road
just lifting

Just so I can stop thinking about it. It is actually boring now I say.
I think I even mean it. Errata say that she definitely didn't lose her
virginity when she was 9 in the treehouse, he just put it in. That
doesn't count does it? We disagree and agree all at once. Since
then, since before I think. In a clammy old garage I looked up in
the sky and whispered to him: Hello boy I say, I wonder where
you are? We write lists of every boy we ever fucked but they blow
away over the balcony into the pool.

Mum and her straight back. Good posture like me, she say.
Ballerina style. She walked up and down with Bird. Bird was 3
days old and knew it, but not much else. My tits were hard as
toads. My daughter is usually as thin as me, say ma. Look at her
now! E-normous! she say. I blink but I am cut in half and can't feel
much else. The dads kept coming in to see the mums. My mum
brought me walnuts. She gave me these cups that go in your bra.
They catch the milk she say. Drip, when your baby cries, they
drip. I won't manage I say. Don't be stupid she say, you just do.
You're not the first woman to have a baby AND YOU CERTAINLY
WON'T BE THE LAST.

I stare at families like they are fish. I watch them drinking tea
from each other. Here and there a man lifts a child high on his
shoulders. Definitely more family than me and my 1.2, the missing
element of husband. Husband. Yes, but is he husband material?

the girls say. I say well yes, he is made of matter – he is *husband substance*. They are bored of my unravelling. The villa is throbbing with chat and the linear equations are all wrong. I am pinned onto the holiday like an example of a badly tied bow-tie, the anti-princess. I am stuck in the cinderella phase, my glass shoe fogged up.

MILF. You're a MILF they say. Thanks I say. Men like it, the milkiness. I am the Lady of the House of Sleep, good and bad. Bird is the real child though, and that upsets them. The magazines say if they love you they will love your child. That's a lie but I haven't the heart to tell 'em. It is bound up with the equations and hard to put a finger on. Love is like time, and people know fuck all about *that*. It moves in the same way and is unreachable. The girls don't believe me, they think I am on the unravel again, childish. I probably am.

driven snow

27/12/05

i remembered the blizzard
surreal now as a fire
there by the door
shaking much
like a tree
was them laughing as i
felt the tugging
as a tide and that
cry like a death
as she entered out from me
snow and blood and sea

climbed inside of me –
a girl
dark as breathing was
living this
presence in flesh
wrapped round me hard
as every year i ever lost
through empty
faces through faces
and unwords was
everywhere like glass she
broke

old bird
white she
blinking in the night
as a star through
the plastic lay bundled
and new not mine
or anyone's
cocoon fresh thing
i stared through
the frost and red cell
shouting of my stomach
at this spine i made
brilliant in the world
as a fact

we'd brought her
to forest in nights
of worlds not found
a compass of flowers
come bright as choirs
thundering
in hands and milk
to air
violent with kissing
this
stillness
and in the eye of
everything
made certain as dying
of love

flora

you, tiny
bundle of right
shining
warm-grubby
like a cut
with milk,
my darkling me
and girl of worlds
i love you in creams
and open space;
your magic eye
and iron stem
are sturdy as dreaming
as excellent, still
i take your mouth
around my breast
to make you
sing of brimming

ⴶ

like christopher robin
you're one sock up
cor blimey! you say
it's a fair cop guv

i have
squared up to the tonka truck
and bare-hand dug
to cupped-up find
your drunken heel
afield with birds

been vast as a girl
a hundred acre wood
to run across
in your flashing trainers

i waited for you in the spinney
to cover your hurt with twiglets –
but we're older now
and the clouds are not animals

Thank you for buying *tunth-sk*. While it is Emma Hammond's first full collection, she has published other work prior this release.

You can find more information on the author at:
http://emmahammond.blogspot.com/

—§—

the waterways series is an imprint of flipped eye publishing, a small publisher dedicated to publishing powerful new voices in affordable volumes. Founded in 2001, we have won awards and international recognition through our focus on publishing fiction and poetry that is clear and true, rather than exhibitionist.

If you would like more information about flipped eye publishing, please join our mailing list online at **www.flippedeye.net**.